THE BRITISH MOTOR INDUSTRY

Jonathan Wood

SHIRE PUBLICATIONS

Published in Great Britain in 2010 by Shire Publications
Ltd, Midland House, West Way, Botley, Oxford OX2 0PH,
United Kingdom.
44-02 23rd St, Suite 219, Long Island City, NY 11101
E-mail: shire@shirebooks.co.uk   www.shirebooks.co.uk

© 2010 Jonathan Wood

Every attempt has been made by the Publishers to secure
the appropriate permissions for materials reproduced in
this book. If there has been any oversight we will be happy
to rectify the situation and a written submission should be
made to the Publishers.

A CIP catalogue record for this book is available from the
British Library.

Shire Library no. 584 • ISBN-13: 978 0 74780 768 1

Jonathan Wood has asserted his right under the Copyright,
Designs and Patents Act, 1988, to be identified as the
author of this book.

Designed by Tony Truscott Designs, Sussex, UK
and typeset in Perpetua and Gill Sans.
Printed in China through Worldprint Ltd.

10 11 12 13 14   10 9 8 7 6 5 4 3 2 1

COVER IMAGE

John Harper Bean (1885–1963) mass-produced his only
model, an 11.9-horsepower car. In 1920 he installed
moving track assembly lines at his factory in Tipton,
Staffordshire, the first British motor manufacturer to do
so. Bean's bid failed and car production ceased in 1929.

TITLE PAGE IMAGE

Welding Austin A50 Cambridge bodies in the West Works
at Longbridge, recorded by artist Robert Johnson – one of
several illustrations he did for a corporate book, *Our First
50 Years*, published in 1955. It declared: 'We await the

future with eagerness and optimism.' Fifty years later, in
2005, car manufacture ceased at Longbridge.

CONTENTS PAGE IMAGE

Austin's Longbridge factory was, thanks to the war,
Britain's largest car plant in 1918. The South Works, to the
right of the railway line, housed production lines; engines
were made in the adjoining North Works, while the West
Works in the left foreground was used for body building.

ACKNOWLEDGEMENTS

Since 1965 I have interviewed hundreds of engineers,
stylists and executives who have helped to shape my views
on the history of the British motor industry. I am
particularly grateful to the following for their
reminiscences although I alone am responsible for any
conclusions reached: John Barber, finance director, Ford
Motor Company and British Leyland Motor Corporation,
and BLMC managing director and deputy chairman;
Sir Terence Beckett, product planning manager and
chairman of Ford of Britain; Ron Lucas, finance director,
British Motor Corporation, and director and treasurer,
British Leyland; Hamish Orr-Ewing, light car planning
manager, Ford, and product planner, Leyland Motor
Corporation; Geoffrey Rose, engineering director, BMC,
and director of planning, Austin Morris division, British
Leyland; Lord Stokes of Leyland, chairman, British
Leyland; John Thornley, general manager, MG Car
Company; Harry Webster, technical director, Standard-
Triumph and Austin Morris division, British Leyland.

Thanks are due to the excellent facilities provided at the
library of the Vintage Sports-Car Club.

I should like to record my grateful thanks to the following
for their help and in providing illustrations: British Motor
Industry Heritage Trust, Tom Clarke, Bruce Dowell, David
Freeth (Singer Owners' Club), Bryan Goodman, Ian
Makins and Peter Seymour (Bullnose Morris Club),
Norman Milne and Dave Whyley (Austin Counties Car
Club) Norman Painting and Graham Robson.

Acknowledgement is due to the Hillman Register (Clive
Baker), Jowett Car Club (Noel Stokoe), Post Vintage
Humber Car Club (Harvey Cook) and the Riley RM Club
(Jacque and Gwyn Morris).

Shire Publications is supporting the Woodland Trust, the UK's leading woodland conservation charity, by funding the dedication of trees.

CONTENTS

BIRTH OF AN INDUSTRY, 1896–1914

BRITAIN'S indigenous motor industry lasted for 109 years. Beginning in 1896 with the formation of the Coventry-based Daimler company, it initially flourished, but deep-rooted faults led to nationalisation in 1975. Though the industry returned to the private sector, MG Rover, Britain's last volume producer, collapsed in 2005. Its remnants are now in the hands of state-owned Chinese car companies. During that period some 1,100 businesses, more than in any other western country, were dedicated to the manufacture and sale of motor cars.

This was an industry that for twenty-three years, from 1932 until 1955, was the largest in Europe and second only to the United States in terms of output. Its demise has been rapid and complete, and today Japan's mainstream motor manufacturers, Nissan, Toyota and Honda, have replaced Britain's indigenous car makers. It all seemed so different in 1896, when the *Daily Telegraph* prophesied: 'We are on the eve apparently of a great engineering departure, similar to that which produced the vast cycle industry 30 years ago…'

Britain's motor industry duly took root and in 1913, the last full year of peace before the First World War, 26,238 cars left the country's factories. This made Britain Europe's second-largest motor manufacturer, behind France, which had produced about 45,000. Germany was a distant third with 17,162. However, the Old World was completely overshadowed by the New, as American output in 1913 stood at 461,500 automobiles completed.

Britain was easily Europe's most affluent market, with 175,300 cars registered in 1913, double the number in France. The motor industry appeared buoyant and self-confident, yet many of its leaders lacked commercial acumen, and this absence of financial awareness was at the root of many a corporate failure. Engineers provided the mainspring of the motor industry but in management they were invariably more preoccupied with the quality of the product than with the bottom line.

It is little wonder that accountants, looked upon as a block on creativity, were reviled figures within significant parts of the industry, and this prejudice

Opposite:
The Model T Ford was Britain's best-selling car between 1912 and 1922; its numerical success is underlined by the front cover of the corporate *Ford Times* of March 1917. A total of 16.5 million Ts were sold world-wide between 1908 and 1927.

Assembling 12/16 Sunbeams at the company's Moorfield Works in Wolverhampton in 1911. Bodies are under construction in the background and were of excellent quality.

The Motor Mills in Sandy Lane, Coventry, had previously been a cotton mill and was empty when the Daimler Motor Company paid £18,000 for the building in 1896. The firm had previously contemplated premises in Cheltenham and Birmingham.

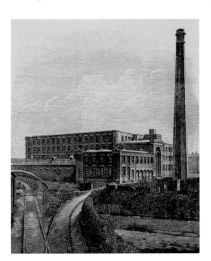

was enduring. As the country's largest car maker of the post-1945 era, the British Motor Corporation did not appoint a finance director until 1965, just three years before its demise.

The British-domiciled, American-owned Ford, and to a lesser extent Vauxhall, with their robust financial targets and limited but highly rationalised model lines, consistently out-performed their British competitors. Even in the post-war years Ford's aspiring engineers were bluntly reminded at interview that their priority was 'to make money for Henry [Ford]'.

Strategy, both technical and marketing, usually reflected the prejudices and whims of the car company's chief executive: what might be described as 'top of the head' thinking. It was 'the cheapest way', said Leyland's Stanley Markland, responsible for transforming Triumph's fortunes in the 1960s, 'providing your head works'. Often it did not.

British engineer managers were invariably the product of a grammar school education but the apprenticeships they served, with their strong emphasis on practical instruction, tended to reinforce the status quo. Many car companies, notably Austin, promoted almost all of their managers from within the business. Until the 1960s a university education was viewed with suspicion and downright hostility by most of Britain's car companies.

By contrast, continental engineers were usually the product of polytechnics and technical universities which, by the nature of their theoretical instruction, challenged convention. This divergent approach became particularly apparent in the 1930s, when many European manufacturers broke with tradition to embrace aerodynamically refined bodywork, front-wheel drive and rear-mounted engines.

Unfortunately, the British public schools, which provided education for the government and civil service, were, consciously or otherwise, overwhelmingly anti-industry. This establishment prejudice against trade was rooted in a classical tradition that regarded money and mechanical labour as vulgar and degrading. The technical education that existed in Victorian Britain did not begin to compare with what was available in Germany. In an attempt to challenge Britain's industrial supremacy, that country had elevated engineering to the status the classics enjoyed in England and as a result engineers enjoyed high social standing.

In the face of such indifference, Britain came late to the motor car. Cars began to be seen on the country's roads during 1895 and the legislation that had effectively prohibited their use was swept away in the following year.

The motor industry's window on Britain and the world was the annual Motor Show, initially held at Olympia, London, between 1903 and 1936. The Adams car in the foreground was built in Bedford from 1906 but its founder, A. H. Adams, perished on the *Titanic* and production ceased in 1914.

This German invention dated from 1886 but was French by adoption, and British cars tended to follow continental designs closely.

Many of the early car makers had previously built bicycles and they invariably bequeathed the strengths and weaknesses inherent in British two-wheelers. Their production, based mainly in the Midlands and London, dominated world trade and soared between 1895 and 1897, when the boom collapsed. The industry had succumbed to cheaper, mass-produced machines from America.

Manufacturers of the most expensive bicycles had made a virtue of producing as much as possible within their factories. This approach affected production methods and Humber, for one, would not countenance the use of automatic machine tools because they were not considered conducive to a 'quality' product. However, many of the smaller manufacturers were reliant on bought-in parts, and specialist component companies began to flourish in response to the bicycle boom. Lucas (from 1878) produced lamps, Dunlop (1896) pneumatic tyres, Brampton Brothers (1852) chains, Auto Machinery (1875) bearings, and Bluemels (1891) accessories. These and many other companies would grow with the popularity of the motor car.

With the downturn in the bicycle market from 1897, Coventry manufacturers such as Humber (in 1898), Rover (1904), Singer (1905), Hillman and Riley (1907) diversified into car production. They also made as much as possible within their own factories. It was an aspiration found throughout the motor industry and embraced by Wolseley, which by 1913 had emerged as Britain's most productive motor manufacturer. In 1914 it claimed to make everything for its cars in its Birmingham works, except for electric coils and tyres. Bought in 1901 by Vickers, it produced about three-thousand cars in 1913 at a considerable loss. Indeed, Wolseley was a copybook example of how not to do it.

Often, however, some components were bought in by car companies although they did not always acknowledge the fact. This contrasted with American practice, and Algernon E. Berriman of *The Auto* magazine reflected entrenched British attitudes when he voiced contempt for transatlantic methods, complaining that 'where companies innumerable are created ... in a night, and start making motor cars the next morning, raw materials are often gearboxes and axles, complete with axle shafts and ball bearings, everything in fact but the oil'. But that was where the industry's future lay.

Following bicycle precedent, British car manufacturers at the cheaper end of the market did produce assembled machines, which, invariably, were of inferior quality. Engines could be bought off the shelf. Initially they came from French De Dion Bouton and then from British firms such as Aster, White & Poppe, Coventry Simplex or J. A. Prestwich.

Birmingham-based Joseph Lucas Ltd began to serve the needs of the motor industry in 1902. This acetylene 'head-light' dates from 1905 and bore the 'King of the Road' name, inherited from the company's bicycle lamps first produced in 1878.

Singer's factory in Canterbury Street, Coventry, built for bicycle manufacture in 1891, became its principal plant when car production began in 1905. The Raglan Street works on the right, previously occupied by Dunlop, was acquired in 1923.

A Wolseley letterhead of 1901 which, in the style of the day, proclaimed the size of its factory in Adderley Park, Birmingham. By 1914 this 3-acre plant had grown sevenfold to cover 21 acres and employed 5,500 people. It was demolished in the 1970s.

The start of Wolseley car production in May 1901, with a 5-horsepower Tonneau model taking shape in a corner of the erecting shop. Note the inverted chassis frames on trestles either side; assembly was then a very static business.

The last was particularly popular during the cyclecar boom of 1910–14. This hybrid, a combination of motorcycle and motor car, was inspired by the French Bedelia. Another continental import was the light car; originating in 1908 and crossing the Channel in 1912, it was defined by having an engine of not more than 1.5 litres capacity.

Such trends were a spur to the component makers, who by 1914 had a significant presence within the industry. Chassis frames came from such businesses as Rubery Owen (1884/1903), Thompson Brothers (1810) and Sankey (1903). E. G. Wrigley (1898) made axles, Dunlop contributed pneumatic tyres and wheels, the latter also being supplied by Rudge-Whitworth (1894), while Guest, Keen & Nettlefolds (1900) produced nuts and bolts. Crankcases were supplied by Birmingham Aluminium (1903), bearings by either Hoffman (1898), Ransome & Marles (1906) or Skefco (1910), and valve springs by Terry's (1913). Renold (1903) and Coventry Chain (1896) made chains.

Carburettors came from Zenith (1909), a subsidiary of the French Rochet-Schneider company, White & Poppe or SU (1904). Electrical equipment was produced by Lucas or Rotax (1906). Clutch and brake linings

A corner of the Wolseley machine shop. Overhead belting that drove the machine tools was a familiar feature of many British car factories until after the Second World War, and was often powered by a gas engine.

were Ferodo's territory (1907), while radiators could be supplied by Peter Serck's Motor Radiator Manufacturing Company established in 1910, the same year as the Moss Gearbox business. S. Smith & Son (1851) responded to an increasing demand for instruments.

But the high-tension magneto, patented in 1903 by Robert Bosch, was a reminder of Germany's command of the global electrical industry. There were hardly any British equivalents, so these sophisticated, precision-made components had to be imported.

While the industrial Midlands was the industry's natural home, London emerged as a secondary location although its car makers tended to be smaller in size and shorter-lived. Talbot (1903), the British arm of French Clement, was located in Ladbroke Grove. In the same year Vauxhall had set up in the district after which it was named, south of the Thames, but in 1905 transferred its business to Luton.

Manchester was home to Rolls-Royce for its first four years. This maker from 1904 of the 'best car in the world' moved to Derby in 1908. As a manufacturer of electrical equipment, Royce & Co made its own ignition coils, and Henry Royce even designed his own carburettors, the cars being so equipped until 1936. The Silver Ghost of 1906 stood head and shoulders above practically all its contemporaries, but if Royce, with his near-fanatical pursuit of perfection, had been responsible for its production it is unlikely that many examples would have ever reached the public.

It took the steadying, perceptive hand of general manager Claude Johnson, the 'hyphen in Rolls-Royce', to refine the company's image. He emerges as the ideal Edwardian manager but, sadly, there were not enough

Dunlop not only made tyres but also accessories. Based at the Para Mills, Aston Cross, Birmingham, the business moved, in 1916, to Fort Dunlop, a 400-acre site then in open country to the north-east of the city.

Small beginnings: the white building in the foreground is the Vauxhall factory at Luton, Bedfordshire, where the company moved from Vauxhall in south London in 1905. Cars would be built at Luton until 2002, while vans are still produced there at the time of writing.

Henry Royce (1863–1933) at the age of forty-four in 1907. The quality of his perfectionist engineering had been recognised by the Honourable Charles Rolls, who sold cars to his fellow aristocrats, and Rolls-Royce Ltd was established in 1906.

like him. Even so, he had a weakness, which was for extravagance. Everything had to be the best. Rolls-Royce's profits were initially modest, rising from a mere £5,389 in 1907 to £91,000 in 1913.

These results also reflected one of Johnson's pivotal decisions, taken in March 1908, namely to discontinue Rolls-Royce's other lines and concentrate solely on the Silver Ghost. At this time most manufacturers were producing a variety of models, aimed at a range of pockets and tastes, which diluted resources and enfeebled the balance sheet. Many British car companies would pursue this misguided policy until the Second World War and, incredibly, Daimler, one of the worst offenders, continued to do so into the 1950s.

A reminder of the devastating effectiveness of the one-model strategy was apparent for all to see. In America in October 1908 Henry Ford discontinued his other lines to concentrate on just one: the Model T. It was destined to be the world's best-selling car until overtaken in the 1970s by the Volkswagen Beetle. Intended from the outset as a world car, the deceptively robust T was launched at the 1908 London Motor Show and assembled from 1911 in a factory in Manchester, which in 1914 introduced a moving track assembly line, Britain's first, at a time when producing a car was a very static affair.

Unlike most of its contemporaries, Rolls-Royce produced just one model, the Silver Ghost, between 1908 and 1921. It did, however, build them only in chassis form. These Ghosts are nearing completion in No. 1 shop at Nightingale Road, Derby, in 1920.

The Ford had not been particularly cheap: on its announcement the four-seater tourer sold for $850 (£175), but in 1914 mass-production contributed to bringing the price down to $550 (£113). In 1913 no fewer than 7,306 Model Ts left Ford's British factory, well ahead of Peugeot, France's largest motor manufacturer, which made some 5,000 cars of varying sizes. The T was thus Europe's most popular car.

Claude Johnson (1864–1926), 'CJ' in Rolls-Royce parlance, and the firm's managing director from 1906 until 1926.

Henry Ford's one-model policy was enthusiastically espoused by Owen Clegg, formerly of Wolseley, who arrived at Rover as works manager in 1911. Though he was to spend only eighteen months with the company, his influence would be felt for the next decade. Like many of its contemporaries in 1911, Rover was offering five unrelated lines, ranging from single- to four-cylinder models. Clegg scrapped them and their replacement was a modern 12, with, briefly, a related 18, which entered production in 1912. To speed and cheapen the production process, it was available in only one

Pictures of Ford's US-style Manchester assembly line are rare. This one, taken c.1915, shows the innovative facility for right-hand-drive Model Ts on the right. Note the dashboards in the foreground.

The popular, reliable and commercially successful Rover 12 of 1912 was destined to survive, in updated form, until 1924. Most were bodied by the works, as in the case of this 'five-seater body'.

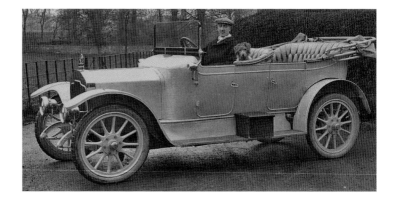

England's first purpose-designed car factory, the Dennis works in Guildford, Surrey, was opened in 1901 and survives as a pub. This architect's drawing is the work of local man John Lake. Dennis ceased car production in 1915 although it still makes fire engines.

colour, pastel green, when a choice of finishes was the norm. The 12 sold for £350 and cost Rover £243 to manufacture. By 1914 it was the only model available.

Some 5,500 examples were sold pre-war and the company's profits rose from a modest £7,100 in 1911 to £137,000 in 1914. This was despite Rover making the majority of the parts within its factory. The success of the 12 ensured that Rover became one of the most profitable businesses in the British motor industry.

Sunbeam, also a manufacturer of bicycles, was another success and its profitability, too, sprang from the influence of one man. In 1909 French graduate engineer Louis Coatalen arrived at its Wolverhampton factory and his 12/16 was one of the best British touring cars of its day. Some five thousand were built between 1910 and 1914. In 1912, it received an updated competition-bred engine, which reflected Coatalen's passion for motor racing. In 1913 Sunbeam's profits stood at £93,409. The Sunbeam works

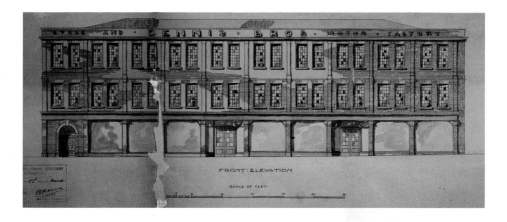

benefited from the latest American machine tools and many British car makers were aware of the superiority of such machinery. Yet they often lacked the knowledge of how to arrange them or how they functioned.

Nonetheless these purchases highlighted the fact that the hub of the world's machine-tool industry had shifted from Britain to the United States. Machine tools were at the heart of the 'American System of Manufacture', which differed from Europe's because of the precision of its interchangeable parts.

It was therefore possible easily to exchange one part with another. The British alternative was to file and fit by hand the component in question but, perversely, its cars were better finished outwardly than American ones, which were often of a more dated design. This gave rise to the notion that such cars were 'cheap and nasty', when in fact their internals were made to a precision unheard of in Britain.

The factories in which these cars were built were usually adaptations of existing engineering premises but some were purpose-built. Again it was the United States with its massive potential market that set the pace, and Henry Ford's Highland Park factory of 1910 was a four-storey structure. By 1915 he had identified the inefficiencies of thus housing the moving track assembly line, and the emphasis switched to single-storey units.

By 1914 Ford had an admirer in Herbert Austin, who in 1905 had left Wolseley, where he had been general manager, to establish a business under his own name at Longbridge, to the south-west of Birmingham. In 1914 he told *The Motor* that 'Cars must be produced in quantities if any profit was to be made'. His profit, averaging £54 per car in 1910–13, was respectable enough.

Ford's Highland Park factory in Detroit, the work of architect Albert Khan, opened in 1910. Setting a worldwide trend for multi-storey plants, it was built to cope with burgeoning demand for the Model T. This photograph was taken in the 1920s, when the complex covered 287 acres.

Gravity-fed Model T wheels are delivered to Ford's moving track at Manchester, c. 1915. This feature was also widely copied throughout the British motor industry, most significantly by Morris (see page 33). Note the modest dimensions of the T's front axle.

In 1914 Daimler also produced half a dozen models and all were powered by sleeve-valve engines of American design. Daimler had managed to make diversity pay, owing to the popularity of the make among the aristocracy after the then Prince of Wales (later King Edward VII) bought one in 1900. In 1910 Daimler built two thousand cars and returned a profit of £100,000. The same year it was bought by BSA, the armaments and motorcycle manufacturer. In 1913 its profits of £187,921 were the highest in the industry.

Herbert Austin's discovery in 1905 of Longbridge, as envisaged by artist Robert Johnson. The empty White & Pike factory had previously been used for making printed tin boxes. Car manufacture began there in 1906 and continued on the site until 2005.

By 1914 sleeve-valve engines, although of a different type to Daimler's, were being offered by Argyll of Alexandria, near Glasgow, produced at the most lavish of all Britain's car factories, which was completed in 1906 at a cost of £220,000. The stone frontage resembled a palatial stately home, giving an inkling of the marbled halls beyond. But overheads demanded mass-production and the cars were built only in modest numbers.

'There are no marbled halls at Cowley and there will never be,' declared William Richard Morris, the chairman of Morris Motors, in 1924. He was a British car maker who had not sprung from a traditional engineering industry background and so was unencumbered by its prejudices. Morris was by far the most progressive British car maker of the pre-1914 era, and his models and manufacturing methods would enable him to become Britain's largest and richest motoring magnate of the inter-war years. Indeed Morris represents the quintessential British success story, having started with nothing, apart from his own ingenuity. A mechanic rather than an engineer, Morris crucially possessed a formidable grasp of finance that belied his modest demeanour.

Above all, he became convinced that 'the best way for the small concerns to manufacture was to get specialists on every separate unit of the job'. This perpetuated the approach he had used as a sixteen-year-old small-time maker of bicycles in 1893, when he bought the parts from component makers and then assembled the machines in a shed in the back garden of his parents' Oxford home.

There was nothing new about building cars in this way. Where Morris differed was that he did not buy ready-made parts. Instead, they were purpose-designed to his requirements, their specifications honed by observation during his years as an Oxford garage proprietor. His aim was to challenge the all-conquering Model T with the two-seater Morris Oxford light car of 1913. Above all, Morrises were not *manufactured* at his Cowley factory: 'We merely *assemble*,' he declared. His approach was the antithesis of the production methods espoused by practically all of his contemporaries. This strategy would be triumphantly vindicated in the 1920s.

William Morris (1877–1963), later Lord Nuffield, was Britain's most successful and richest car maker of the inter-war years. This photograph of him was distributed to his sales outlets during the 1920s. Between 1926 and 1960 he donated £25.7 million to mainly medical charities.

MORRIS LEADS THE WAY, 1918–29

IN THE 1920s Britain's motor industry got into its stride and flourished. In 1923, the first year in which the industry separately recorded car production, a total of 71,396 vehicles left the country's factories. Output increased annually until 1929 and that year attained 182,347 units. In Europe only France built more, delivering some 211,000 cars in the same year. A record number of new companies appeared, eighty-six between 1919 and 1925, although market forces ensured that by 1929 the total figure had dropped to forty-two.

Motoring was still confined to the middle and upper classes. And cars were changing. In 1919 the typical British motor car was a four-seater open tourer. In 1929, a vehicle's occupants were enjoying the comfort and protection of a saloon. Like so many trends, this idea originated in the United States. The Hudson-owned Essex pioneered the concept of making the closed car cheaper than the open one, which it achieved in 1926. The trend soon reached Britain and by the end of the decade some 85 per cent of new British cars were saloons.

The small six-cylinder engine grew in popularity. By 1929 it had overhauled the four and usually employed coil ignition. This cheap American invention had by then succeeded the magneto, despite the wartime creation of Britain's own industry, established when supplies of German-made Bosch units ceased.

The ranks of the proprietary engine manufacturers were swollen by the arrival of Henry Meadows (1920); Coventry Simplex became Coventry Climax in 1917, while British Anzani (1912) also came to the fore.

As some manufacturers began to recognise the folly of trying to make as much as possible within their own plants, the number of component makers grew. Engine blocks now came from Midland Motor Cylinder (1915), gears and gearboxes from ENV (1919), steering boxes from Marles (1919), universal joints and propeller shafts from Hardy Spicer (1912, so renamed in 1926), while Autovac (1920) supplied fuel systems.

Triplex (1922) made safety glass, and Alford & Alder (1925) manufactured front-wheel brakes. In 1926 Lucas gained a monopoly of

Opposite:
Joseph Lucas's factory in Great King Street, Birmingham, dates from 1890. It was much enlarged during the First World War when supplies of German-made Bosch magnetos ceased and home production began. This photograph shows a still significant workforce in the depression year of 1930.

A modest start: a partially completed Morris Oxford in the newly built body shop at Cowley, c.1920. In that year Morris built just 1,994 cars but by 1923 the figure had leapt to 14,995, overtaking Ford, and making him Britain's largest car maker.

During the inter-war years motoring was an essentially middle-class pursuit. Here a family is enjoying a day out in their 1924 Bean 14, built at Tipton, Staffordshire. This strong, reliable model also generated a following in Australia, where its robust qualities were much appreciated.

electrical equipment when it took over both Rotax, renowned for producing the best components in the business, and the ailing C. A. Vandervell.

American interests were represented by General Motors-owned AC (1920), which made sparking plugs. The distinctive sound of the 1920s horn was provided by Klaxon (1921). Bendix (1927) produced brakes, and until 1935 T. B. Andre manufactured Hartford shock absorbers and Silentbloc bushes under licence.

By far the most significant American presence was Pressed Steel, founded in 1926, in which the Edward G. Budd Corporation of Philadelphia held a controlling interest. It had pioneered the pressed all-steel body in the States. William Morris helped establish it in Britain but he withdrew in 1930 so that the company could accept orders from rival manufacturers. Once established at Cowley, opposite the Morris works, it could rapidly supply uniformly stamped bodies, replacing the labour-intensive handmade ones. However, the dies to produce the panels were expensive and required a significant production run to recoup tooling costs.

The cars built by Britain's motor manufacturers in the 1920s were affected by two pieces of protectionist legislation aimed at stemming the flood of cheap American cars into the country. During the war, in 1915, the Chancellor of the Exchequer,

A consignment of Sankey artillery wheels, widely used by the motor industry throughout the 1920s, leaving the Hadley Castle Works of Joseph Sankey at Wellington, Shropshire. Acquired by steel maker John Lysaght in 1919, that business was in turn absorbed by GKN in 1920.

Reginald McKenna, had introduced 'McKenna Duties', which subjected such imports to a 33.3 per cent tariff. Following pressure from the motor industry, they were renewed after the war and remained in place (except in 1924–5) until 1967, when they were modestly relaxed. Britain's car makers were fearful of an 'American invasion', worrying that they would suffer like the bicycle industry had twenty years before. Therefore any American or continental car maker which wanted to sell its vehicle in Britain could do so only by establishing a factory, as Ford had done, on British soil.

General Motors had in 1909 established a depot at Hendon, where it had imported its cars in CKD ('completely knocked-down') form from Canada (a British dominion – so reducing the duty payable). A similar ploy was adopted by Chrysler, the last member of the American 'Big Three', which in 1924 took over premises at Kew. Hudson's presence on the Great West Road out of London dated from two years previously.

In the United States the dominant Model T was being challenged by General Motors' Chevrolet, together with the more expensive Buick,

The Firestone tyre factory by night. Opened on the Great West Road at Brentford, Middlesex, in 1928, it was designed in the Art Deco style by Wallis, Gilbert & Partners but was summarily demolished over the 1980 August Bank Holiday.

The horsepower tax dominated British engine design between the wars. This Austin Seven unit has 56-mm bore, which produced an RAC rating of 7.8 horsepower, so this popular little car was actually an Eight.

There were few British factories untouched by the First World War. Here French Clerget and Le Rhône aero engines have been reconditioned by Herbert Engineering of Reading, Berkshire. The firm went on to produce the HE car from 1919 until 1931.

Oldsmobile and Cadillac lines. In 1925 GM purchased Vauxhall, which hitherto had been unprofitably producing high-quality cars. In 1924 it had built some 1,500 but thereafter the strategy would be geared for higher-volume, lower-cost models for the mass market.

In 1926 Citroën, France's most productive car maker of the decade, opened an assembly plant at Slough. In the following year Renault followed suit with a facility at Acton. In 1928 Fiat did likewise at Crayford, Kent.

The second piece of protectionist legislation came in 1921: the so-called 'horsepower tax', by which motorists paid a graduated Road Fund Licence based on the RAC horsepower rating of their cars' engines. Set at £1 per horsepower, this formula was applied to penalise big-bored, large-capacity American cars, such as the Model T Ford. Rated at 22.5 horsepower, it cost £22 a year to tax while the owner of the British 11.9-horsepower Morris Cowley paid just £12. However, the tax had a profound impact on the design of British car engines. They were soon displaying narrow bores and long strokes in an effort to keep the RAC rating of their engines as low as possible.

Four years of hostilities had shaped the structure of the motor industry. Practically all car companies had seen their businesses expand dramatically as a consequence of war work, whether munitions, tanks, aero engines or aircraft. The insatiable demands of conflict saw a streamlining of manufacturing methods and the bespoke items of the pre-war era gave way to uniformity. In consequence the derogatory term 'mass production' entered the language.

Morris had learnt much from the assembly of mine-sinkers during the war and calculated that he could build one of his Bullnose cars in six days. The distributor paid for it 'at the factory gate', either in cash or by banker's draft. Morris had obtained six weeks' credit from his suppliers, who were always paid promptly, so generating their loyalty. The fortunes of Morris Motors were built on this simple but effective formula.

In 1925 Morris became the first British car maker to record a seven-figure profit, with a pre-tax surplus of £1.5 million. In that year 47,138 Bullnoses left the company's Cowley factory, representing 36 per cent of total British car production. This was mainly due to the success of the Cowley model. In 1915 William Morris had introduced this larger car, which was able to accommodate a family of four. Under the bonnet was an imported 1.5-litre American engine, for which he paid $85 (£17 14s) apiece. Coventry-based White & Poppe's estimated price had been about £50.

When the war ended, Continental, its manufacturer, decided to discontinue the engine but Morris was able to acquire the rights and get Hotchkiss, which had established a machine-gun factory in Coventry in 1915, to copy it. When in 1923 it was unable to keep pace with demand, Morris bought the business, having already acquired his body supplier in the city. Such acquisitions fragmented Britain's largest car company and by 1939 Morris was running twelve factories scattered around Oxford and the industrial Midlands. They included Wolseley, which after two loss-making decades was acquired in 1927.

Following his purchase of the Hotchkiss plant, Morris had appointed an outstanding production engineer, Frank Woollard, as its manager. In 1924 he introduced a fully automatic transfer machine, the first in the world, to machine gearbox casings and flywheels. Unfortunately, it was let down by ancillaries and was in due course dismantled. Woollard's pioneering work highlighted the increasing importance of the production engineer within the British motor industry.

Morris's great rival of the inter-war years was Sir Herbert Austin (knighted in 1917), although much of the content of his cars was produced at his single manufacturing facility. In 1921 a financial crisis led to a receiver being installed at Longbridge and Austin was forced to appoint Carl Engelbach as his works director and production engineer. Austin was stubborn in personality but could be pragmatic under pressure. He was a competent although conservative engineer but the crisis had exposed his fiscal deficiencies. He therefore bowed to his bank and his creditors, and Ernest Payton, a Lloyd's underwriter

A Daimler lorry and trailer heading a line of vehicles loaded with a day's supply of Morris engines about to leave Hotchkiss's factory in Gosford Street, Coventry, for Cowley, 50 miles to the south. The plant became Morris Engines in 1923.

The Austin Seven of 1922 was initially available only in touring form but by the end of the decade saloons were in the majority. This prep school scene of 1930 is a reminder that cars, even small ones, were for the better off.

and businessman, became finance director and, in 1928, Austin's vice-chairman. It was a key appointment.

Sir Herbert had followed Ford by adopting, in 1919, a one-model policy. His 3.6-litre 20, inspired by the Model T, proved to be too large; it was a victim of the horsepower tax and the depression that ravaged the country in 1921. He quickly scaled down the design and produced the Austin 12 for the 1922 season. Well-built and dependable, if pedestrian, it survived until 1935. Also produced in taxi form, the 12 was to be a familiar sight on the streets of London well into the 1950s.

Austin's most famous model was small and unplanned, funded from his own pocket in the face of opposition from his co-directors. The Seven of 1922 was a large car in miniature, and its tiny 747cc engine the smallest-

In 1926 Austin's production engineer, Carl Engelbach, embarked on a radical reorganisation at Longbridge, this being completed in mid-1927. In the foreground is the conveyor which brought engines, in this instance 12-horsepower units, to the chassis assembly shop.

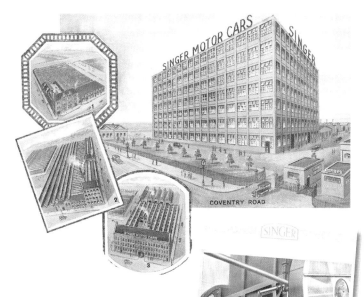

capacity British four-cylinder unit on the market. Enduring until 1939, it overtook the 12 in 1926 to become the most popular Austin model.

By 1929 Austin and the larger Morris concern were the twin pillars of the British 'Big Three'. The final member was Singer, and their combined output constituted 75 per cent of British car production. Singer would never again attain such heights and a significant factor in its undoing was the choice of an unsuitable factory. Some engineering companies had followed the example of Henry Ford's first factory and built multi-storey facilities. One of these was BSA's former small-arms works at Small Heath, Birmingham, which Singer bought in 1927. The purchase and equipment cost £750,000. It proved to be a white elephant. Singer's managing director, W. E. Bullock, then embarked on an increasingly complex model programme. This culminated in Singer losing £200,000 in 1935 and becoming one of the also-rans.

The 700-ton Bliss press that cost Singer £17,000 to purchase and transport from America. Installed in its Canterbury Street factory in Coventry, it had many functions but, as shown here, was principally used to stamp chassis side members.

The purchase of an over-large factory also played its part in the demise of Clyno, a Wolverhampton car company that made the mistake of shadowing Morris's strategy. It was established in 1922 by motorcycle manufacturer Frank Smith, who was reputed not to price his cars until he had viewed

The MG of 1924, a special-bodied Morris Oxford, took its name from the Morris Garages, the first of which opened in Longwall Street, Oxford, in 1910. Happily its frontage survives, a reminder of the days when Morris Motors was the city's largest employer.

Cowley's list. The Clyno was a sound, assembled job; in 1926 the company had its best ever year and produced 11,149 cars, about a quarter of Cowley's output. Then, in 1928, Smith erroneously believed that Morris was planning a £100 car and responded with the Century, a bargain-basement version of the 9-horsepower model. It sold for £112 but the financial burden so imposed, together with the cost of a new 70-acre works in the Wolverhampton suburb of Bushbury, caused Clyno to collapse in 1929.

Such were the changing fortunes of the mass producers. At the other extreme, Rolls-Royce's Claude Johnson had in 1922 launched a smaller car for the owner driver, the 20 horsepower, which was to outsell the Phantom I, the Silver Ghost's replacement. A significant contribution to Rolls-Royce's net profit of £185,768 in 1929 came from the sales of its aero engines, 22 per cent of turnover and rising, their production having begun during the war.

In the dark days of 1921 Rolls-Royce had toyed with the idea of producing a small car like the 10/15 Humber. A deeply conservative

The ground-breaking ceremony for Ford's factory in Dagenham, Essex, took place on 16 May 1929. Sir Percival Perry, who was to direct Ford's British operations until 1948, is in the foreground. Henry Ford's son, Edsel, is on the left, and behind him, to the right, is his eleven year-old son, also Henry.

company, Humber fell into deficit in 1928 and was absorbed into the Rootes brothers' growing empire. They were cost-conscious car salesmen rather than manufacturers, strongly influenced by General Motors' manufacturing strategy. Rootes Ltd had become Britain's largest car distributor, and the dynamism of its chairman, Billy Rootes, was checked only by his more cautious brother, Reginald. On acquiring a majority shareholding in Humber in 1928, Rootes then took over a faltering Hillman, its next-door neighbour.

General Motors was also the inspiration for STD Motors of 1920, an unwieldy Anglo-French combine which took the shine off Sunbeam's pre-war status following its alliance with Talbot and Darracq. Louis Coatalen's passion for motor racing absorbed precious resources and in 1924 STD was forced to issue £500,000 worth of guarantee notes redeemable ten years later.

Performance and reliability were the keynotes of the Bentley, Britain's most famous sports car of the 1920s. Dating from 1919 and made in north London, Bentleys five times won the 24-hour race at Le Mans, and, when enhanced with formal coachwork, they challenged Rolls-Royce's and Daimler's dominance of the carriage trade.

There was also the well-engineered Coventry-built Alvis (1919). Aston Martin (1921) was in business at Feltham, Middlesex, from 1927 onwards. Nearby, at Staines, was Lagonda (1906), the product of a ramshackle collection of corrugated iron sheds built in its founder's back garden.

All of these cars made little or no money. An exception was MG (Morris Garages), the creation of its general manager, Cecil Kimber. Unusually, he combined a gift for styling with a talent for works organisation and a flair for good financial housekeeping. Dating from 1924, the first generation of MGs comprised special-bodied Morris Oxfords, and the M-type, announced in 1928 and costing £175, was to sell 3,235 examples. Mainly produced at the company's new Abingdon factory, it was the world's most popular sports car and would tide MG over the worst excesses of the Depression, which began in October 1929.

Hillman adopted a one-model policy in the 1920s and its 14 was available between 1922 and 1930. The Coventry marque was taken over by the Rootes brothers in 1929 and became one of the big sellers of the following decade.

CRESSWELL

MARCH OF THE BIG BATTALIONS, 1930–45

ALTHOUGH the 1930s have been characterised as a decade of industrial depression, motor manufacturing consolidated its position as one of the buoyant new industries of the inter-war years. This was no more apparent than in Coventry, whose population grew by 35 per cent, from 167,083 in 1931 to 224,267 in 1939.

Thirty-three car companies existed in Britain in 1939, a result of the economic downturn and the emergence of the six mass producers. In order of output they were: Morris, Austin, Ford, Vauxhall, Rootes, and Standard. This compared with a 'Big Three' in both the United States and France, Germany's 'Two' and Italy's singleton, Fiat.

During the 1930s the lines became more sharply drawn between Britain's indigenous motor manufacturers and the more efficient, cost-conscious American ones. In 1939 the combined pre-tax profits of Ford and Vauxhall amounted to £2.9 million, while the *total* surplus recorded by the remaining four major British car companies stood at £3.2 million, just £300,000 more.

This was in part due to most of the principal native car manufacturers offering an increasingly wide range of models. In 1934 Austin listed no fewer than fifty-one and most of these were being matched by Morris. One of the worst offenders was Riley. Although its distinctive sports saloons were sufficiently good to survive the Depression, a large and growing variety in the late 1930s contributed to a collapse. A takeover in 1938 by William Morris (now Lord Nuffield) added yet more factories to his sprawling empire.

The effects of the Depression of 1929 only briefly affected Britain's main car makers and although output fell in 1930–2 it rose again in 1933 to 220,779, some 38,000 more than the previous high of 1929. Production thereafter increased year on year to peak in 1937 at 389,633, more than double the 1929 figure.

There were casualties among the smaller, more vulnerable companies. In 1931 loss-making Bentley was bought by Rolls-Royce, the same year in which BSA acquired Lanchester, one of the industry's founders, for it to reappear as a cheaper line to the larger, more expensive Daimlers. Aston Martin and

Opposite: Britain's first unitary construction car, the Vauxhall 10 of 1938, drawn by Leslie Cresswell for *The Light Car* magazine. Built up from welded pressings, the engine/gearbox unit and independent front suspension were carried on a sub-frame.

Lagonda found salvation from wealthy backers, respectively shipping magnate Sir Arthur Sutherland in 1933, and corporate wheeler-dealer Alan Good in 1935.

Invicta was another victim of the Depression. But Noel Macklin, its instigator, pragmatically reinvented it as the Railton Eight of 1933 by the use of cheap American mechanicals, namely imported Hudson chassis, cloaked in English coachwork. The result was a potent, cost-effective sporting car which, unlike its predecessor, made money for its sponsor.

In 1932 Britain overtook France as Europe's largest car maker, and in 1935 France was also overhauled by a resurgent Germany, led since 1933 by Adolf Hitler. As early as 1935 the British government believed that a war with Germany was inevitable, prompting its 'shadow factory' scheme to mass-produce Bristol aero engines.

The motor industry would manage new plants that were financed by the Exchequer. Most were built adjoining the manufacturers' own factories. Three members of the 'Big Six', Austin, Rootes and Standard, together with Daimler and Rover, were each paid a £50,000 annual management fee and £75 per engine, the first of which was delivered in 1938.

Car-manufacturing processes were streamlined and a technological milestone was marked in 1937 with the introduction by GM's Vauxhall of its new 10-horsepower model, the first British-made car to feature monocoque construction. The absence of a chassis made the car lighter than hitherto, but high volumes and a limited model range with long production runs became essential to recoup tooling costs.

As mass production came to predominate, the component companies grew in size and significance. This trend was exemplified by Automotive Products (1920), which was a perceptive licensee of American components.

Austin's Eight was a typical British saloon of the 1930s, still with side-valve four-cylinder engine, separate chassis and all-round half elliptic springs. Independent front suspension would not feature on most makes until after the war. Introduced in 1939, the Eight survived until 1948.

In 1928 came AP-made Lockheed hydraulic brakes, followed by the Borg & Beck clutch (1931) for which even Rolls-Royce became a customer in 1936, the Purolator oil filter and the Thompson steering joint.

The New Hudson Brake Company's Girling rod in tension brakes also attracted significant customers in the shape of Austin, Ford, Riley and Rover. The business was bought in 1943 by Lucas.

Businesses were combining. In 1936 Birmid Industries was formed to include Birmingham Aluminium, Midland Motor Cylinder and Stirling

'I never realised . . . *that a clutch meant so much.'*

What does our intense specialisation on clutches mean to the motorist?

It means (1) a sweet-acting clutch, light in touch, that starts the car gently and helps to make gear changes smoother

(2) a trouble-free clutch, giving long service with practically no attention

(3) a sweet-running car, due to the Borg & Beck power-smoothing device

(4) outstanding success in clutches. We have already made 600,000 at Leamington Spa

BORG & BECK
THE CLUTCH THAT MEANS SO MUCH

BORG & BECK COMPANY LIMITED, TACHBROOK ROAD, LEAMINGTON SPA, ENGLAND

Humber was the first British manufacturer, in 1932, to fit Automotive Products' Borg & Beck clutch. Previously most manufacturers had made their own clutches but this one became increasingly popular throughout the industry in the 1930s.

Right: Making headlamps at Lucas's Birmingham factory. The workforce stood at 8,380 in 1930, when this photograph was taken, women being in the majority. Some can be seen operating the machines in the background.

Below: Automotive Products opened its Leamington Spa factory in 1932 and one of its principal licensed products was the Lockheed hydraulic brake, adopted by Triumph in 1925 and, more significantly, by Morris-owned Wolseley in 1929.

Metals. Hardy Spicer became allied in 1938 with Laycock Engineering of Sheffield, which also built propeller shafts, under the umbrella of Birfield Industries.

The early 1930s were difficult years at Cowley and it was not until the arrival in 1934 of the Eight that Morris Motors regained its form. It was launched by Leonard Lord, its combative new managing director, aged only 36, an outstanding production engineer who had proved his worth at Morris Engines. Lord was destined to play a dominant role in the affairs of the British motor industry until his retirement in 1960.

Owing to the success of the Eight, some 218,000 examples of which would be built by 1938, Morris's fortunes were again in the ascendancy, but Lord, the architect of its success, had departed, sacked by Lord Nuffield in 1936 following a liaison with a young female employee. When Lord did return to the industry in 1938, it was as heir apparent to the ageing Lord Austin, ennobled in 1936. Smouldering with resentment, Lord pledged to 'tear

Cowley apart brick by bloody brick'. This was a particularly telling comment because in 1933–4 he had transformed Morris's factory into a showpiece capable of producing 120,000 cars per annum.

Austin had begun the decade in good form, having introduced a 10-horsepower model in 1932 which was to become its best performer. The Seven had sold well during the Depression years and output peaked with the appearance of the Ruby saloon in 1935. In 1939 Austin's profits stood at £664,000 but lagged way behind Morris's, which were nearly three times more at £1.9 million.

The most significant achievement of the 1930s came from the Rootes brothers, who transformed the fortunes of Hillman and Humber through a programme of ruthless rationalisation. Hillman was the engine of growth and the Minx family saloon of 1932 was a strong performer in the dominant 10-horsepower sector. Using the American motor industry as his example, Billy Rootes pruned the Hillman range to this one model, although some low-volume sixes were available from 1931.

Contemporaries were quick to dismiss Billy and Reginald for being salesmen rather than engineers, but that was precisely why they succeeded. Their empire was further expanded in 1935 when STD Motors defaulted on its 1924 guarantee notes and Sunbeam and Talbot were brought into the

One of the chutes used to deliver tyred wheels to the four chassis assembly lines at Cowley in 1934, a consequence of Leonard Lord's £250,000 upgrading of Morris's assembly facilities. It was then able to produce two thousand cars during a forty-hour week.

Humber's status as the choice of the affluent middle classes is underlined in this advertisement also intended to appeal to the socially ambitious.

H U M B E R   L I M I T E D   C O V E N T R Y

London Showrooms and Export Dept.: Rootes Ltd., Devonshire House, Piccadilly, W.I
London Service Depot: Somerton Road, N.W.2

The Rootes brothers, Billy (left) and Reginald, were, as they often quipped, respectively engine and steering and the brakes of the Rootes Group. But the dynasty only briefly survived into its second generation, succumbing to a takeover by Chrysler in the 1960s.

Rootes orbit. A new marque, Sunbeam-Talbot, was born in 1938 and in the following year Rootes's profits stood at a record £330,000.

Another new contender in the mass-production market was Standard, established in 1903. It had lost £18,000 in the buoyant year of 1929 but was reinvigorated by the mercurial John Black. In the 1920s he had run Hillman with his brother-in-law, Spencer Wilks. With the Rootes takeover, he went to Standard and Wilks to Rover. In 1936 Black introduced the 'Flying' Standards, which by 1939 embraced a range from 8 to 20 horsepower. With an output that year of some 55,000 cars, its profits of £318,000 were the highest of the decade.

These four British companies now had a formidable competitor in the shape of a revitalised Ford. Despite the 22-horsepower Model T having been replaced in 1928 by the similarly unsuitable A, the Ford Motor Company had decided to dispense with its Manchester factory. In 1931 it opened a purpose-built plant at Dagenham, Essex, on the lines of its mighty Rouge River facility in Detroit.

This highly integrated plant was capable of producing 120,000 cars a year, had a self-contained power station and could manufacture its steel. A greater contrast to Morris's scattered empire is difficult to imagine. However, in the American manner Dagenham lacked a body plant, so a branch of Briggs Motor Bodies, established in Detroit in 1909, opened nearby in 1932. Unfortunately the new works had little to build, apart from the unsuitable Model A car and truck. So Detroit rapidly designed the 8-horsepower Model Y and by 1934 it had gained a significant 54 per cent slice of British 8-horsepower sales. Indeed Morris's Eight had been produced in response to it.

The Ford Eight and the mechanically related Ten constituted Dagenham's volume sellers of the decade, and the highly rationalised nature of the range was underlined in 1939 when this business, which had made a loss in 1931–2, made record profits of £1.78 million, only £138,000 behind Morris, the market leader.

In 1939 Ford had built 48,031 cars while Vauxhall, owned by its General Motors rival, made 34,367. In 1930 Vauxhall had produced only 1,277 and during the decade built more of its Bedford trucks than cars. As with Ford the 1939 volume sellers were related and consisted of a 10 and a 12.

In 1931, during the worst of the Depression, a new make, SS, emerged, founded by William Lyons, one of the few global figures produced by Britain's motor industry. Not an engineer but a stylist of international stature, he was fiscally astute and effectively his own finance director. He possessed an innate sense for marketing and was an ardent advocate of rationalised production.

Because Lyons lacked financial resources, the first generation of models were essentially rebodied Standards but from 1935 onwards the SS Jaguar sports saloons from Coventry combined looks with performance at a market-

Ford's factories usually adjoined navigable water so that iron ore could be shipped in and cars out. Dagenham, opened in 1931, was no exception and its Thames-side quay is readily apparent. Behind it is the plant's power station, which burnt London's rubbish.

sensitive price. The same also went for the lower-volume sports cars although Lyons instinctively favoured the more popular saloons as key providers of turnover and profit. In 1939 SS built 5,378 cars and recorded a net surplus of £48,787, the equivalent of £5 16s per car.

That year Rover built 11,103 cars, about twice as many as Jaguar, and its net profits of £205,957 equated to an impressive £18 11s per car (Austin made £5). By then favoured by bank managers and country solicitors, the company had failed to find a viable replacement for Clegg's 12. Fortunately, in 1929 it was reinvigorated by Spencer Wilks and his brother, Maurice, who had learnt his rationalised engineering in 1926-8 with General Motors. However, Rover's revival would not have been possible without the contribution of chartered accountant H. Howe Graham. He ran the company in the years 1932-3, when its future hung in the balance, and, although Spencer Wilks took over as managing director, Graham remained on the Rover board. He was its chairman from 1954 until his retirement in 1957.

Graham had, however, been unable to save Triumph, another Coventry bicycle maker which had begun building cars in 1923. In the 1930s its management took its products up-market in an overcrowded sector and filed for bankruptcy in 1939.

Rolls-Royce was impressed with the products of Rover and SS but it had taken time to adjust to the death in 1933 of Sir Henry Royce, and the last model to be built regardless of cost was the V12-powered Phantom III of 1936. From 1938, the perceptive works director, Ernest Hives,

Assembling cars at Dagenham in 1936. In the foreground is a standard 8-horsepower Fordor Model Y, with a 10-horsepower CX, about to receive its body, behind. These were produced by Briggs Motor Bodies at its nearby plant, opened in 1932, which in 1953 was taken over by Ford.

addressed the question of soaring manufacturing costs and initiated a rationalised range of four-, six- and eight-cylinder engines, although their impact would not be apparent until after the war. With hostilities in the offing, aero engines contributed 94 per cent of the £1.2 million profit Rolls-Royce recorded in 1939.

A Rolls-Royce was the chosen transport of H. F. S. (Harry) Morgan, who in 1910 had begun producing at Malvern Link, Worcestershire, his three-wheeled cyclecar, a concept that,

THE 1½ LITRE SALOON

incredibly, survived until 1952. This talented engineer, unusually for the profession, had a sound grasp of finance. This explains why Morgan has been one of the industry's great survivors. In 1936 Morgan had introduced the 4/4, his first four-wheeler, and its spiritual successors survive to this day, their styling still rooted in the 1930s.

The 4/4 was selling against Cecil Kimber's MGs. Kimber's careful stewardship of the 1920s gave way to a proliferation of models and a successful racing programme. A cumulative profit of a mere £419 in the years 1930–5 saw MG's independence curtailed in 1935; racing was scrapped, the range greatly simplified, and design now centred on Cowley rather than Abingdon. Volumes and profitability duly increased.

MGs were exported the world over, albeit in small numbers, but the overwhelming majority of British-built cars stayed at home. Partly owing to protectionist legislation, this was an introspective industry that produced cars with small, long-stroke engines, low gearing and unyielding suspension, and which were unsuited for use overseas.

Exports peaked in 1937 when 78,100 cars were dispatched; 68 per cent of the total value went to preferential Empire destinations, where British cars were favoured by expatriates living in Australia, New Zealand and South Africa. There they were mostly selling against cheaper, reliable and larger-engined American cars, often enhanced with independent front suspension. Their manufacturers reaped the benefits of volume production, so reducing the unit cost of individual vehicles by selling essentially the same model at home and abroad. It was a lesson that British car makers would ignore at their peril in the years that followed the war.

William Lyons created lines that could never be mistaken for another make. The performance of the Coventry-built SS Jaguar 1.5 litre for 1938 was enhanced by the fitting of the Standard-based engine with a Weslake overhead-valve cylinder head.

CARS FOR WORLD MARKETS, 1945–58

THE LACK of civilian vehicle production throughout the Second World War and the full employment that followed it generated a pent-up demand for motor cars. The 1950s were a seller's market for the industry, and car production in Britain all but doubled between 1950 and 1958, rising from 522,515 units to 1,051,551.

In a bid to raise precious currency for an economy bankrupted by war, the post-war Labour administration directed the car makers to sell their products overseas, despite their unsuitability. Sports cars were an exception to this, and the open two-seaters from Abingdon and Coventry found a ready and growing export market, particularly in the United States.

With Britain's continental rivals devastated by conflict, this was a perfect opportunity to transform what was essentially a parochial industry into one with global ambitions. A buoyant export market would have resulted in rising volumes, providing the product was right, and a reduction in unit costs. The bait was steel supplies, which were geared to overseas sales. Initially, and with little competition, British exports soared, although at the expense of the home market. In 1950 no fewer than 66 per cent of new cars were sold overseas.

To encourage the motor men to produce larger-engined cars more suited to foreign markets, the government abandoned the horsepower tax after twenty seven years, to be replaced in 1948 by a flat rate. It also pointed out the need for the native motor industry to abandon its wasteful multifarious lines and adopt a one-model strategy. These entreaties were met, at best, with mixed responses.

The car makers could now expand into the former shadow factories they had managed during the war. Austin, Daimler, Jaguar, Rolls-Royce, Rootes, Rover and Standard were all to benefit from these new facilities.

A government diktat of 1947 required that the industry should not expand in its industrial heartland but had to do so in areas of high unemployment, such as South Wales, Merseyside and Scotland.

Opposite:
As a result of the shortages created by the war, the 1950s were a seller's market for Britain's car makers. A Park Ward-bodied Rolls-Royce Silver Wraith touring saloon is in the foreground at the 1954 Motor Show at Earls Court, where the show had moved in 1937.

The post-war export drive is well represented by these Austin A40 Devons, being loaded on board a ship. No fewer than 47,000 of the first 50,000 of this model, introduced in 1948, went abroad, mostly to the United States. But the overwhelming majority of British cars proved to be unsuitable for overseas use.

The working class was now joining the ranks of car owners. Before the war motor manufacturing had been a seasonal business, peaking in the autumn and winter and falling off in the summer. Now it became a year-round activity and with it came labour problems. A turning-point came in 1956 when BMC laid off one in eight of its workers, without notice and with no redundancy pay. Strikes, both official and unofficial, were to become the norm.

The government-sponsored Motor Industry Research Association of 1945 advised motor manufacturers on how to improve the quality of their products, particularly for world markets. Here MIRA's banked test track at Linley, Warwickshire, is undergoing construction in 1951.

The MGA roadster, introduced in 1955, was followed by this coupe version in 1956. As the left-hand steering indicates, this example was destined for America, where the overwhelming majority of As were sold. The wire wheels were a popular optional extra.

Jaguar's sports cars also found a ready market in the United States. It began with the 3.4-litre XK120 in 1948 and this was the last of that line, the XK150 of 1958. Left-hand drive and whitewall tyres underline this example's transatlantic destination.

The Nuffield Organisation, as the Morris empire was renamed during the war, with its multitude of plants was particularly vulnerable in this regard. However, in 1948 it did at least possess the world's finest small car in the Morris Minor. Its creator, Alec Issigonis, an immensely talented engineer/artist, had ensured that it was not only distinctive in appearance, but also the first British car to handle well. Unfortunately, the ageing Lord Nuffield hated its appearance but it was a car tailor-made for the

Cowley comes to Canada: the Beaver tribe meets a Morris Minor, a car that looked like no other. Exported to many parts of the world, Alec Issigonis's outstanding model never made the same global impact as the Volkswagen Beetle.

BMC's badge, current between 1952 and 1968, was a rosette in appropriately patriotic colours. Like his motor industry contemporaries, the Sir Williams Lyons and Rootes, Leonard Lord was also a dedicated farmer. His inspiration was the insignia from awards made at agricultural shows.

government's export drive. While Minors were sold abroad, overseas sales could be maintained only by an ongoing policy of refinement. But a myopic management, parochial by nature, lacked the vision to raise its eyes beyond the home market. With a takeover by Austin in the offing, Issigonis left Cowley for Alvis in 1952 just as the British Motor Corporation came into being.

Its chairman, Leonard Lord, with his barely disguised contempt for Cowley's products, saw no reason to support the Minor even though it was BMC's best-selling model of the 1950s and was profitable to the tune of £40 a car. Even so it became the first British model, in 1961, to sell a million examples, but its great export potential, and the economies of scale that went with it, were largely unrealised.

Instead, the world, and particularly America, embraced the Volkswagen Beetle. This initiative of Hitler was inspired by Ford's one-model policy and designed by Porsche for global markets. In 1956 Britain ceded its dominance of European production to West Germany, mainly through the success of the Beetle, having forfeited its global export lead in the previous year.

With the formation of BMC the Big Six became five and brought Britain's two largest indigenous car companies, Morris and Austin, within single ownership, with 40 per cent of the market. Less happily, Morris, MG, Wolseley and Riley came with a multiplicity of factories.

In truth the businesses were never to be fully integrated. Crucially, that element of financial control and accountability which had been the hallmark of Lord Nuffield's stewardship of Morris Motors was subjugated to Lord, an intuitive, decisive executive, but one who lacked a grasp of corporate finance. Neither was he capable of a coherent marketing strategy; indeed, one of his oft repeated axioms was 'Build bloody good cars and they sell themselves'.

Lord had become Austin's chairman in 1946, following the death of financier Ernest Payton, and engineers then dominated the Longbridge board. Ruthless, paranoid and running BMC through fear, Sir Leonard, as he became in 1954, effectively sacked his most able lieutenant, works director Joe Edwards, over pre-lunch drinks one day in 1956. This left Lord's amiable but pliant deputy, George Harriman, as his heir apparent.

Lord had initiated a new make, the Austin-Healey of 1952, which became BMC's corporate sports car. One of the marques to emerge after the war, Donald Healey's Riley-engined cars were fast but expensive and heavy. Demand was patchy and, realising that he would soon go out of business, he came up with the lighter, cheaper Austin-powered Healey 100, which became the first Austin-Healey.

However, BMC already owned MG, which had to continue with its pre-war T-Series sports cars until Lord gave approval for the Abingdon drawing office to be reopened in 1954, thanks to the persuasive powers of its general manager, John Thornley.

The famous Riley engine was distinguished by its high-performance hemispherical combustion chambers with inclined valves actuated by short pushrods from twin camshafts, rather than the more expensive twin overhead type. Created by Percy Riley in 1926 and revised in 1936 by Hugh Rose, it survived in 2.5-litre form until 1958.

Austin's CAB (Car Assembly Building) 1, completed at Longbridge in 1951, was chairman Leonard Lord's masterpiece. Here it is the subject of a BBC television outside broadcast in 1953 with an Austin A40 Somerset saloon in the foreground and a rare convertible version behind.

Leonard Lord (1896–1967) dominated the British motor industry from 1933 until his retirement as chairman of BMC in 1960. He was known by his workforce as 'Lord Foulmouth' on account of his colourful language.

The Austin-Healey was BMC's corporate sports car and this 2.6-litre 100/6 dates from 1958. The Riley One Point Five on the right, together with its Wolseley 1500 stablemate, was designed at Longbridge and started life as a Morris Minor replacement.

The outcome in 1955 was the 1,489cc MGA, the work of Syd Enever, another engineer/stylist in the Issigonis tradition. In due course over 100,000 would be built, making it the world's most popular sports car. Over 80 per cent were sold in the United States. The 1,798cc MGB, its 1962 successor, did even better, with over half a million produced. But this figure was distorted as the problems that were to engulf BMC in the 1960s meant that the model had to soldier on until 1980.

The greatest challenge to BMC came from Ford, which in 1951 introduced its closely related Detroit-designed four-cylinder Consul and six-cylinder Zephyr saloons. These, together with the smaller 100E of 1954 and, amazingly, the pre-war-based Popular, which continued to sell, constituted the entire Ford programme. That year 210,153 cars left Dagenham, providing Ford with a profit of £19.01 million. Although BMC produced some 120,000 more cars, they were spread over many more models and factories and its surplus of £17.9 million was some £1.1 million less than Ford's.

Ford's robust chairman, Sir Patrick Hennessy, was held in high regard by the Ford family, who accordingly allowed Dagenham a degree of autonomy

not apparent in its other subsidiaries. Above all, Ford England was changing.

Following Detroit's example, and so directed in 1948, initially against his better judgement, Hennessy introduced a policy of graduate recruitment. One such was twenty-seven year-old Terence Beckett, an economist *and* engineer, who joined Ford in 1950. In 1951 he became Hennessy's personal assistant. A new breed of Ford executive was in the making, to plan, analyse and evaluate.

Unlike Ford, Vauxhall was more closely tied to American control but Luton's model range resembled Dagenham's in the shape of the four-cylinder Wyvern of 1951 and the related Velox, a six.

In 1957 Rootes recorded a deficit of £567,000, a reflection of the Suez Crisis and the labour problems that were afflicting the industry. Standard, another Coventry company, directed by Sir John Black (knighted in 1943), had in the meantime grown through acquisition by buying moribund Triumph in 1945. His motivation was to challenge William Lyons's sports cars.

Had Standard been wholly reliant on its cars, it would probably have succumbed to a takeover, even in the booming 1950s, as Singer fell to Rootes in 1956. But Black took over the production of the lightweight TE21 Ferguson tractor. This was an agricultural implement for the world, the government gave its backing and Standard's profits benefited accordingly. Standard also lent itself to a rationalised approach because when in 1948 it

Irish-born Sir Patrick Hennessy (1898–1981) was arguably Britain's outstanding motor industry executive of his day. He held the demanding position of purchasing manager of Ford's British operations before becoming managing director in 1945. He was its chairman between 1956 and 1968.

Although Ford's six-cylinder 2.3-litre Zephyr of 1952 was a popular saloon, Carbodies of Coventry was responsible for this factory convertible conversion of 1953, available until 1956. Employing electro-hydraulic operation, the hood could be partially unfurled in the 'coupé de ville' position.

take a good look when it passes you

introduced the Vanguard, an unworldly world car, its engine was extended to the Ferguson and later used in the TR sports-car line of 1953. The board, faced with an increasingly erratic Sir John, had had enough. Under pressure from his co-directors, Black resigned as managing director in 1954, and his place was taken by a relative, Alick Dick.

Elsewhere in Coventry, William Lyons had discarded the

Above: The anonymous car was the 1.5-litre Jowett Javelin of 1947–53. It was a brave but ill-fated attempt by an under-capitalised Bradford-based company to produce an advanced, modern car, styled and engineered by former Morris engineer Gerald Palmer.

Below: The sporting two-door 1.4-litre Sunbeam Rapier hardtop of 1956 was derived from the Hillman Minx family saloon, and Rootes charged £985 for it, some £280 more than the Minx. The visually enhanced Rapier II of 1958 allowed the model to assume its own identity.

tarnished SS name and replaced it with that of Jaguar. In 1950 he launched the Mark VII, a long-planned 100-mph saloon. Its 3.4-litre twin overhead camshaft XK engine had already been used in the XK120 sports car. It also powered Jaguar's C- and D-type sports racers, which gave the company five wins at Le Mans and echoed Bentley's successes of the 1920s.

Yet Sir William, as he became in 1956, looked to the 24-hour race merely to provide publicity for the company's mainstream saloon lines; a secondary 2.4-litre model had appeared in 1955. Not so David Brown, who in 1947 had bought the Aston Martin and Lagonda companies and was determined to win the classic event. Aston Martin finally did so in 1959.

Rover, now resident at its Solihull shadow factory, continued to provide transport for the affluent middle classes. In 1948 and with a million-square-foot works to occupy, the Wilks brothers, inspired by the wartime Willys Jeep, had conceived the idea of a Rover for the farmer. Again with government encouragement, the Land Rover was precisely the type of product the post-war world was awaiting. Its rugged

William Lyons (1901–85), Jaguar's chairman, photographed in 1948 before he regularly wore spectacles. The intercom unit on his office desk allowed him to speak to his senior staff, regardless of whether they were on the telephone or not.

Standard's Sir John Black (1895–1965) with the 2-litre Vanguard, produced in 1948 In response to the government's one-model policy. Stylistically inspired by the American Plymouth saloon, the car, alas, was more suitable for the home market than the intended world one.

47

One of Britain's legendary engines, Jaguar's twin overhead camshaft XK unit was produced between 1948 and 1992. Suitable for saloons and sports cars, this example, sectioned and burnished for exhibition purposes, is on display at the 1954 Motor Show.

Opposite top: Rover's four-wheel-drive Land Rover of 1948 found a ready market throughout the world. At home the AA's yellow-painted Solihull-built vehicles were a familiar sight on Britain's roads in the 1950s.

specification, coupled with the quality of Rover engineering, ensured a global customer base.

Rolls-Royce, now located at Crewe, Cheshire, continued to produce its cars in chassis form only. The arrival in 1955 of the Silver Cloud and Bentley S-type, which shared a common Pressed Steel body shell, symbolically marked the end of the bespoke coachbuilt body.

By this time Rolls-Royce was principally a manufacturer of aero engines and this also applied to Bristol, which in 1947 launched its own car, built to aircraft quality standards. The Bristol 400 was a German model in all but name, being based on pre-war BMW engineering, an assured combination of the 328 engine, 326 chassis and 327-derived body.

Colin Chapman's new Lotus marque was Diametrically opposed to the Bristol. The first of the line, an Austin Seven-engined special, led to the Mark VI of 1953, a multi-tubular space-frame club racer, which gave way to the Seven in 1957.

Below: The aerodynamically refined Bristol 400 of 1947 was based on BMW components, thanks to the efforts of its pre-war UK concessionaire H. J. Aldington (right). He is seen here at the Bristol Aeroplane Company's Filton factory with Italian racing driver, Count 'Johnnie' Lurani.

The seller's market in Britain was essentially satisfied by the end of the decade, but crucial changes were taking place in the industry's structure. With the exception of Vauxhall, the motor manufacturers were reliant on external contractors for their body supply. Ford, fearing that Chrysler would buy Briggs in America and so control its body supply, was able to buy Briggs's British subsidiary in 1953. BMC followed suit with its purchase of Fisher & Ludlow. Of the smaller companies, David Brown acquired Tickford and BSA purchased Carbodies, which built London's taxis. This left still-independent Pressed Steel as the country's largest body manufacturer.

BOOM THEN BUST,
1959–74

THE 1959 Motor Show at Earls Court was the most significant since the first post-war event in 1948. It featured three saloon models, all outstanding in their ways: the Mini from BMC, the Ford 105E Anglia, and Standard-Triumph's Herald. Of these the Mini was by far the most significant technically. For the first sixty or so years of its existence the British motor industry had eschewed technical innovation in the continental idiom. Instead, it opted for a policy of gradual refinement on established themes.

Alec Issigonis had joined BMC in 1955 and his front-wheel-drive Mini was so revolutionary in concept that it has changed the way in which the world designs its cars. Alas, his extraordinary creativity was matched by arrogance and insularity. He had demanded a completely free hand in the Mini's design, a luxury that he had not enjoyed when he conceived the profitable Morris Minor. As a consequence, the ingenious, ground-breaking Mini was expensively over-engineered to an unacceptable degree. BMC, its manufacturer, believing that the public would be fearful of such a revolutionary concept, compounded the error by underpricing it. The cheapest version of this technological *tour de force* sold for £496, which was £93 less than Ford's new but wholly conventional 105E Anglia.

Such was the public demand for the 848cc Mini and its similarly underpriced but technically advanced derivative the 1100, that BMC attained a 35 per cent share of the British market in 1965. But George Harriman, who became chairman in 1961 and together with Issigonis effectively ran the business, was an engineer in the Leonard Lord mould.

As a consequence BMC exemplified the accountant's cautionary maxim of 'turnover vanity, profit sanity'. Outward success masked an inbred management, their inadequacies often concealed by arrogance, a lack of forward planning, multifarious outdated factories and simmering labour problems. Above all, the radical but empirically costed move to front-wheel drive was a significant factor in the Corporation tumbling into deficit in 1967. By 1965 its profit-per-car figure had slumped to £20, half that recorded in 1955.

Opposite:
De Luxe Minis in the CAB 1 facility at Longbridge in the early 1960s. They were also produced in CAB 2, opened in 1961. The latter was part of BMC's plan to increase annual output to one million vehicles but the highest figure it attained was 730,862 in 1964.

Ford had in the meantime followed a technically conventional route. The 997cc Anglia was not only all new with nothing carried over from previous models, but it was the first Ford to be designed in Britain at a facility the company had established in Birmingham in 1956.

In 1955 Dagenham, uniquely for a British car company, embraced Product Planning, a concept that emanated from Ford's parent. It removed the

Left: Alec Issigonis (1906–88), the most influential engineer in the post-war British motor industry. Responsible for the Morris Minor and the Mini, he is seen here at Buckingham Palace in August 1969, having just received a knighthood from the Queen.

Below: No car more characterised the vitality of the 1960s than the Mini, which combined the road-holding attributes of front-wheel drive with inspired packaging for four occupants. This is a 1965 example. The Mini survived until 2000 with sales totalling 5.3 million.

AUSTIN Incredible **mini** Saloon....

★ Combined ignition/starter switch.
★ Safety sun visors and interior mirror.
★ Two-leading-shoe brakes at front.
★ Greater torque capacity gearbox.

...now with Hydrolastic suspension

Lord Nuffield in 1962 with Alec Issigonis's newly introduced, technically advanced Morris 1100, destined to be the best-selling British car of the 1960s. But, like the Mini, it was under-priced, a shortcoming that would never have occurred in Nuffield's day.

programme of model development from the chief executive, where it had been subject to his hunches and whims. In addition cost estimators now sat next to the design engineers to eliminate expensive mistakes before they happened. Such a process was the reverse of Issigonis's inspirational but fiscally undisciplined approach.

The result was the impeccably costed 1,200cc Ford Cortina of 1962, 'a large car at a small car price'; a light, front-engine, rear-drive family saloon which also found a ready market as a corporate fleet car. Ford sold one million Cortinas in four years and the line survived until 1982. By then it had contributed approximately half of Ford car profits.

The 105E Anglia of 1959 with its distinctive reverse-rake rear-view window (cheaper to manufacture than a conventional one), was the first British-designed Ford, although styling was by the American Elwood Engel. The Anglia continued in production until 1967 and over one million were built.

The Ford Cortina was a strong export performer and here Mark I cars are awaiting dispatch overseas. In August 1963 Ford announced it had shipped 312,000 cars in the previous 12 months, then a record for a British motor manufacturer.

The most expensive car of the 1959 show trio was the Triumph Herald, a brave attempt by Standard to produce a car after its body manufacturer, Fisher & Ludlow, had been bought by BMC. Therefore chief engineer Harry Webster designed a model that reverted to a chassis so that its body parts, made by smaller press shops, could be brought together like a jigsaw puzzle. Styling was crisply individual, the work of the Italian Giovanni Michelotti, and the Herald was also offered with all-independent suspension for £702.

Even before the 948cc Herald could get into its stride, a credit squeeze in 1960 threw Standard into the red and it was bought by the Lancashire truck maker Leyland. This was a business dating from 1897, built on the twin pillars of robust no-nonsense engineering and sound financial housekeeping. Leyland's Stanley Markland transformed Triumph, cutting costs and initiating a new executive saloon, the Michelotti-styled 2000, which drove Triumph's return to profitability. Markland, one of the unsung heroes of an industry in dire need of competent, cost-conscious

Sir Terence Beckett (knighted in 1987) joined Ford as a graduate recruit in 1950 and went on to head its innovative Product Planning section, triumphantly vindicated by the commercial success of the Ford Cortina line. Beckett was chairman of Ford of Britain from 1976 to 1980.

Left: Triumph's Herald of 1959 endured until 1971. This is a 1961 example of the improved 1,200cc version. The model was also known for its excellent lock, making it popular with lady motorists, and the idea of Standard director Martin Tustin, previously Ford's first product planning manager.

Below: Ford's factory at Halewood on Merseyside was opened in 1963, the result of a government directive. In 2008 ownership passed to Tata Motors. The Jaguar X-type ceased production there in 2009 although the Land Rover Freelander continues to be built.

William Munger Heynes (1903–89), Jaguar's accomplished chief engineer from 1935 until 1969. A pivotal advocate of the XK engine being a twin-cam unit, Heynes had overall responsibility for a succession of outstanding Jaguars, including the E-type shown here.

The forced smiles say it all. BMC's chairman Sir George Harriman (left) and Sir Donald Stokes, his opposite number at the Leyland Corporation, announce, against the backdrop of bitter negotiations, the formation of British Leyland on 17 January 1968.

executives, departed in 1966 when he failed to be appointed Leyland's chairman. That job went to the company's go-getting sales director, Sir Donald Stokes.

A rival to Triumph's 2000 was Rover's wholly new saloon of the same name and, with Land Rover sales buoyant, the company under the Wilks regime emerged as one of the best-managed businesses within the British motor industry. In 1967 it also succumbed to a Leyland takeover, following BMC's purchase in 1965 of Pressed Steel, Rover's body supplier. Jaguar was another customer and the move also unsettled the cautious, pragmatic Sir William Lyons.

As a consequence, in 1966 Jaguar was acquired by BMC on the understanding that Lyons would be left to his own devices. It was a good match. The Corporation mass-produced small front-wheel-drive cars and Jaguar manufactured lower-volume sports saloons.

In 1960 Jaguar had bought Daimler from BSA and in the following year launched the E-type, effectively a road-going version of the Le Mans-winning D-type and Britain's most outstanding sports car. But Lyons, however, was far prouder of the XJ6 saloon of 1968, a case study in refinement, stylistic and mechanical excellence, all for £2,253.

If the affairs of BMC dominated the headlines, Rootes also got its fair share, having suffered from government directives. In 1963 it opened a new factory at Linwood, Scotland, for the manufacture of its new, technically advanced small car, the rear-engined Hillman Imp, which was plagued with reliability problems. It was a factor in the American

Chrysler Corporation taking a 30 per cent stake in the business in 1964, consolidated by an outright takeover three years later. Casualties were Singer (1970), Humber and Sunbeam (1976), followed by Hillman in 1978, all being replaced by those of Chrysler.

Vauxhall should have boomed in the 1960s but a succession of clearly American-inspired designs saw the company wilt in the face of opposition from Ford and BMC. Subsequently, in 1974, General Motors accorded its stronger Opel subsidiary responsibility for the design of all its European cars and Vauxhall became a purely manufacturing operation. GM's initiative followed that of Ford, which in 1967 had united its British and German arms to form Ford of Europe, although Britain continued to play a significant design role.

That year Jaguar achieved a profit of £1.1 million, when BMC made its first ever loss, of £3.2 million. The Labour government of the day, concerned that a key industry was being directed by an ailing chairman in Sir George Harriman (knighted in 1965) who was not up to the job, encouraged Leyland, headed by Sir Donald Stokes, to take over the business.

This occurred in January 1968, when the British Leyland Motor Corporation was formed. It was soon to be headed by Stokes, who was unaware of the depth of BMC's malaise. Engineers, who had dominated management hierarchy, were replaced by one of the country's best-known salesmen. The entire indigenous motor industry now came within a single organisation and in 1971 British Leyland held a commanding 40 per cent of British new car registrations. But Riley and Austin-Healey disappeared in 1969 and 1971.

The first six-cylinder Triumph sports car was the TR5 model briefly built in 1967/8. These examples coming off the line at the company's factory at Canley in Coventry were destined for America, where the model was sold as the TR250.

British Leyland's 1100/1800 Austin Allegro replaced the Issigonis-designed top-selling 1100/1300 in 1973 but was manifestly inferior to its predecessor. This is the Allegro II of 1976. Its sales failure marked the beginning of the end of Britain's indigenous motor industry as a volume producer.

Gordon Bashford, responsible for the layout of every post-war Rover, with his last car, the V8-engined SD1 hatchback of 1976. On the right is a 1937 10-horsepower Rover, a model on which Bashford worked after joining the company in 1930.

In 1972 the British motor industry recorded its highest ever figure of 1.9 million cars produced. That year the Ford Mark III Cortina emerged as Britain's best-selling model, having finally usurped Issigonis's Morris/Austin 1100/1300. British Leyland's replacement was the egg-shaped Austin Allegro of 1973, a car that was manifestly inferior to the model it succeeded.

Issigonis had been sidelined with the Leyland takeover and replaced by Triumph's Harry Webster, who was responsible for the Allegro, while ex-Ford stylist Harris Mann had executed its lines. Its failure marked the beginning of the end of Britain as a volume producer of cars.

Industrial disputes that had begun in the BMC years now accelerated under Donald Stokes (Lord Stokes since 1969). He was unwilling to contemplate much-needed factory closures because of the threat of industrial action from the trade unions. Strikes were in any event endemic and a consistently overmanned Leyland was now building some of the worst-designed and worst-built cars in the industrialised world.

The deeply flawed Allegro strengthened the hand of the deputy chairman, ex-Ford finance director John Barber. He believed that the 'only world class companies within British Leyland were Rover and Jaguar' and had argued from the outset that the company should have moved its products up-market. Investment, to the tune of £95 million, was therefore switched to Rover. A new factory was built at Solihull for the production of the big 3.5-litre SD1 saloon, the locomotive that was intended to haul British Leyland into sustained profitability. Then in 1973 the Arab–Israeli war broke out and oil prices soared, triggering a global recession. To Stokes's dismay, 'everyone stopped buying expensive cars in order to buy the ruddy Mini again', which was still loss-making.

The company was reaching the limit of its overdraft. In December 1974 the Labour government intervened to guarantee its bank loans and in June 1975 British Leyland was nationalised, being renamed Leyland Cars. Although car making would survive in some shape or form until 2005, this was effectively the end of Britain's indigenous motor industry, exactly eighty years since motor cars had first been seen on the country's roads.

In a spate of factory closures, the MG plant at Abingdon shut in 1980, having been there since 1929. Here MGBs are under construction in the final year of production.

The British Leyland badge of 1968–75 was derived from the earlier Leyland Corporation motif but with the letter 'L' added to its hub.

EPILOGUE:
1975 TO DATE

Of the myriad mainstream companies that once constituted the British motor industry, only MG and Rover survived into the twenty-first century. They were united in 2000 with the creation of MG Rover Ltd, a business that lasted until 2005.

LEYLAND Cars survived until 1978, when its new chairman, Michael Edwardes, renamed it BL Cars. A move up-market saw the business become the Rover Group in 1986, and the company returned to the private sector in 1988 when it was purchased by British Aerospace. After 1975 there were no more Wolseleys, while the last Morrises, Triumphs and Austins were built in 1983, 1984 and 1989 respectively.

In 1994 the Group was acquired by BMW but in 2000 it was sold, for a token £10, to the British-owned Phoenix Consortium. What became MG Rover survived until 2005. However, BMW retained the Mini brand and launched the new MINI from a Cowley factory in 2001.

In the meantime Jaguar had been privatised in 1984 and was bought in 1989 by Ford, which had already acquired Aston Martin in 1987. In 2000 it purchased Land Rover from BMW, but, with its parent company facing soaring deficits in America, Ford disposed of Aston Martin in 2007 to a consortium, while Jaguar and Land Rover passed in 2008 to the Indian Tata Motors. Ford car production at Dagenham had ceased in 2002 although the plant continues to produce diesel engines for a worldwide market.

In 1978 Chrysler UK was bought by Peugeot. It closed the Linwood plant in 1981 but continued to run the former shadow factory at Ryton-on-Dunsmore near Coventry until it too closed in 2007.

Vauxhall car production ceased at Luton in 2002 although van assembly continues there; Ellesmere Port, Cheshire, opened in 1963, is now its only British car plant.

Aero-engine manufacturer Rolls-Royce, bankrupted in 1971, hived off its car-making facility and was bought in 1980 by Vickers, which disposed of the business in 1998. The Bentley marque and the former shadow factory at Crewe went to Volkswagen, while BMW acquired the Rolls-Royce name and transferred production to a purpose-built plant near Goodwood, West Sussex.

Legislation aimed at limiting trade union power, introduced in 1982 by Margaret Thatcher's Conservative government, encouraged the Japanese Nissan company to open a factory at Washington, County Durham, in 1986.

BMW produces its MINI at the former Pressed Steel plant originally established at Cowley in 1926 and completely modernised for the start of production in 2001. Here final assembly is taking place.

After BMW took over the production of Rolls-Royce cars in 1998, it built this partially underground factory, its roofs topped with grass, near Goodwood, West Sussex. It opened in 2003 and is capable of producing a thousand cars a year.

With Britain a member of the European Economic Community, its products were thus given preferential access to European markets. Honda and Toyota followed suit in 1992.

Lotus is today the property of the Malaysian Proton company but London Taxis International, successor to Carbodies, purchased in 1973 by Manganese Bronze, is still in British hands. The same goes for Bristol, owned since 2001 by enthusiast and entrepreneur Toby Silverton, while Morgan,

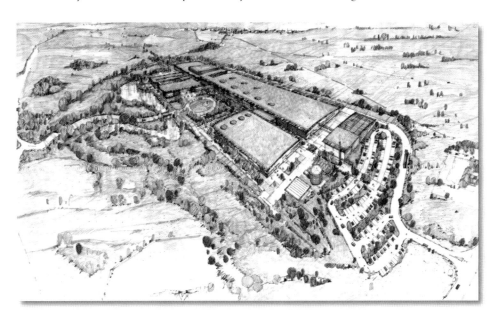

New order: Nissans have been built at Washington, County Durham, since 1986. It is Europe's most productive car factory, with 101 vehicles produced annually per employee.

The end of the road for Rover. A 600 model undergoes frontal deformation tests at the Motor Industry Research Establishment's Crash and Protection Centre at Linley, Warwickshire.

built on the twin pillars of engineering and cash-consciousness, remains in the ownership of its founding family. Today the overwhelming majority of cars sold in Britain are imported from Europe with the balance built within these shores by foreign manufacturers. Those failings so apparent at the industry's birth in 1896 have remained remarkably enduring.

FURTHER READING

Adeney, Martin. *The Motor Makers*. Collins, 1988.

Collins, Paul, and Stratton, Michael. *British Car Factories from 1896*. Veloce, 1993.

Georgano, Nick; Baldwin, Nick; Clausager, Anders; and Wood, Jonathan. *Britain's Motor Industry: The First Hundred Years*. G. T. Foulis, 1995.

Georgano, Nick (editor). *The Beaulieu Encyclopedia of the Automobile* (two volumes). The Stationery Office, 2000.

Turner, Graham. *The Leyland Papers*. Eyre & Spottiswoode, 1971.

Wood, Jonathan. *The Motor Industry of Britain Centenary Book 1896–1996*. Eclat Initiatives, 1996.

Wood, Jonathan. *Wheels of Misfortune: The Rise and Fall of the British Motor Industry*. Sidgwick & Jackson, 1988.

PLACES TO VISIT

There are well over a hundred transport museums of varying sizes throughout the British Isles which contain a good selection of British cars of all ages. It is always advisable to check before making a visit. They include:

Coventry Transport Museum, Millennium Place, Hales Street, Coventry CV1 1JD. Telephone: 024 7623 4270. Website: www.transport-museum.com

Glasgow Museum of Transport, 1 Bunhouse Road, Glasgow G3 8DP. Telephone: 0141 287 2720. Website: www.glasgowmuseums.com

Grampian Transport Museum, Montgarrie Road, Alford, Aberdeenshire AB33 8AE. Telephone: 01975 562292. Website: www.gtm. org.uk

Heritage Motor Centre, Banbury Road, Gaydon, Warwickshire CV35 0BJ. Telephone: 01926 641188. Website: www.heritage-motor-centre.co.uk

Lakeland Motor Museum, Holker Hall, Cark-in-Cartmel, Grange-over-Sands, Cumbria LA11 7PL. Telephone: 01539 558328. Website: www.lakelandmotormuseum.co.uk

Llangollen Motor Museum, Pentre Felin, Llangollen, Denbighshire LL20 8EE. Telephone: 01978 860324. Website: www.llangollenmotormuseum.co.uk

Manchester Museum of Transport, Boyle Street, Cheetham Hill, Manchester M8 8UW. Telephone: 0161 205 2122. Website: www.gmts.co.uk

National Motor Museum, John Montagu Building, Beaulieu, Brockenhurst, Hampshire SO42 7ZN. Telephone: 01590 612345. Website: www.beaulieu.co.uk

Ulster Folk and Transport Museum, Cultra Manor, Holywood, County Down BT18 0EU. Telephone: 028 9042 8428. Website: www.nmni.com/uftm

INDEX